DATE DUE

JUN 2 0 2012			

What's in the NORTHEAST?

By Lynn Peppas

Crabtree Publishing Company

www.crabtreebooks.com

Crabtree Publishing Company

www.crabtreebooks.com

Author: Lynn Peppas
Publishing plan research and development:
   Sean Charlebois, Reagan Miller
   Crabtree Publishing Company
Proofreader: Crystal Sikkens
Editorial director: Kathy Middleton
Photo research: Crystal Sikkens
Designer: Ken Wright
Production coordinator: Ken Wright
Prepress technician: Ken Wright
Print coordinator: Katherine Berti

Cover description: Harvard University is the oldest center for higher learning in the United States. The Statue of Liberty is located on Liberty Island in New York Harbor. A lobster boat loaded with traps is shown leaving Maine Harbor. Niagara Falls in New York serves as the International border between Canada and the Unites States.

Title page description: The United States Capitol is located in Washington, D.C., at the top of Capitol Hill. It is the meeting place for the United States Congress.

Photographs:
Dreamstime: page 9
iStockphoto.com: page 19 (inset)
Shutterstock: Olga Bogatyrenko: page 25 (top);
   S. Borisov: page 7; Adriano Castelli: page 16
   (right); Zhong Chen: cover (top right), page 19
   (bottom); Anthony Correia: page 29 (bottom);
   Songquan Deng: page 24; Vlad Ghiea: page 25
   (bottom right); ibsky: page 10; iofota: page 16
   (left); Gina Jacobs: page 12; David Kay: page 21
   (inset); Jeff Kinsey: page 28; Lissandra: title page;
   Sepavo: page 18, 23, 27 (inset);Victorian
   Traditions: page 29 (top); Vsevold33: page
   27 (bottom)
Wikimedia Commons: Jason Safoutin: page 13;
   Jim Hood: page 20 (inset); jkb: page 21 (bottom);
   Doug Kerr: page 22; Ad Meskens: page 25
   (bottom left); Fordmadoxfraud: page 26
Wikipedia: Engraving by W. Roberts: page 17
   (Emancipation Proclamation)

Illustrations:
Samara Parent: pages 4–5, 6, 8, 11, 20
Bonna Rouse: page 15
Margaret Salter: pages 14, 17

Library and Archives Canada Cataloguing in Publication

Peppas, Lynn
   What's in the Northeast? / Lynn Peppas.

(All around the U.S.)
Includes index.
Issued also in electronic formats.
ISBN 978-0-7787-1824-6 (bound).--ISBN 978-0-7787-1830-7 (pbk.)

   1. Northeastern States--Juvenile literature. I. Title.
II. Series: All around the U.S.

F4.3.P46 2012   j974   C2011-904843-4

Library of Congress Cataloging-in-Publication Data

Peppas, Lynn.
   What's in the Northeast? / Lynn Peppas.
     p. cm. -- (All around the U.S.)
   Includes index.
   ISBN 978-0-7787-1824-6 (reinforced library binding : alk. paper) -- ISBN 978-0-7787-1830-7 (pbk. : alk. paper) -- ISBN 978-1-4271-8778-9 (electronic pdf) -- ISBN 978-1-4271-9596-8 (electronic html)
   1. Northeastern States--Juvenile literature. I. Title. II. Series.

F4.3.P47 2012
974--dc23
                                 2011026691

Crabtree Publishing Company
www.crabtreebooks.com   1-800-387-7650

Printed in Canada/082011/MA20110714

Published in Canada
Crabtree Publishing
616 Welland Ave.
St. Catharines, ON
L2M 5V6

Published in the United States
Crabtree Publishing
PMB 59051
350 Fifth Avenue, 59th Floor
New York, New York 10118

Published in the United Kingdom
Crabtree Publishing
Maritime House
Basin Road North, Hove
BN41 1WR

Published in Australia
Crabtree Publishing
3 Charles Street
Coburg North
VIC 3058

CONTENTS

Welcome to the U.S.A. 4

The Northeast Region 6

Landforms 8

It's a Waterful Region 10

The Climate 12

The First Peoples 14

Coming to America 16

Population Distribution 18

Natural Resources 20

Economy and Industry 22

Tourism 24

The Northeastern Culture 26

Art, Architecture, and Famous People 28

Timeline 30

Find Out More 31

Glossary and Index 32

Words that are defined in the glossary are in **bold** type
the first time they appear in the text.

Welcome to the U.S.A.

The United States of America is the world's third-largest country in size and population. It is in the North American continent and shares a **border** with two other countries—Mexico to the south, and Canada to the north. From sea to shining sea, the United States has two water boundaries—the Pacific Ocean to the west, and the Atlantic Ocean to the east. The country is divided into 50 different states and one district. Alaska is the largest and most northern state. The smallest is Rhode Island on the eastern coast. The country's capital is Washington, District of Columbia.

What are Regions?

From coast to coast, the United States can appear quite different from one area to the next. For example, an American in Alaska lives in a very different landscape and **climate** than an American living in Arizona. For this reason, the nation is divided into different regions. A region is an area that has one or more common characteristics or features.

AK

OR

CA

In God We Trust

The national motto is "In God We Trust." It is found on the country's coins and paper money.

HI

Why are Regions Needed?

Regions are made to help people understand and describe an area. A region can be a very small area, such as a neighborhood, or a very large area that stretches for many miles. Regions share characteristics such as politics, economy, culture, climate, landforms, vegetation, population, natural resources, or wildlife. Regions can be created from almost anything you can think of!

The Five Regions

In this series the United States is divided into five different regions. They are the Northeast, the Southeast, the Midwest, the Southwest, and the West. These regions are made up of states that are close together. The states in a region share common features such as history, landforms, and natural resources. This book explores the common features of the Northeast region of the United States.

The Northeast Region

The Northeast region is made up of two smaller **subregions** called New England and the Mid-Atlantic states. The New England states are Connecticut, Rhode Island, Massachusetts, Vermont, New Hampshire, and Maine. The Mid-Atlantic States include Delaware, Maryland, New Jersey, New York, Pennsylvania, and the District of Columbia. When looking at a map of the United States the Northeast region is found in the northeast, or top right, corner of the country.

Northeast Borders

The northernmost border of the Northeast region is Canada, and the easternmost border is the Atlantic Ocean. Virginia and West Virginia are to the south of the Northeast region, and Ohio is to the west.

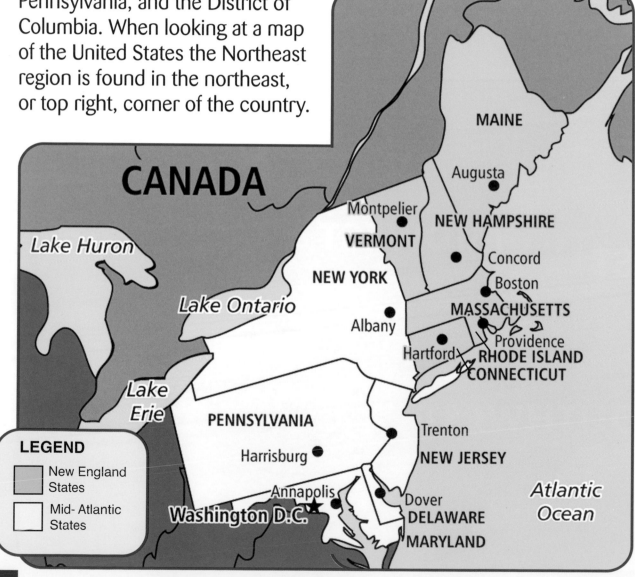

Oldest

European settlers came to the Northeast shore of the United States in the early 1600s to **colonize**. These early colonies later became some of the country's first cities and towns. Cities such as Albany, New York, Plymouth, Massachusetts, and Jersey City, New Jersey, were settled in the early 1600s. Gloucester, Massachusetts, is known as "America's oldest **seaport**."

Big and Small

New York is the largest city in the United States. More people live there than any other U.S. city. Other large American cities are in the Northeastern region such as Philadelphia, Pennsylvania, and Boston, Massachusetts. The Northeast's state of Rhode Island is the smallest state in area in the United States. It has an area of 1,214 square miles (3,144 sq. km).

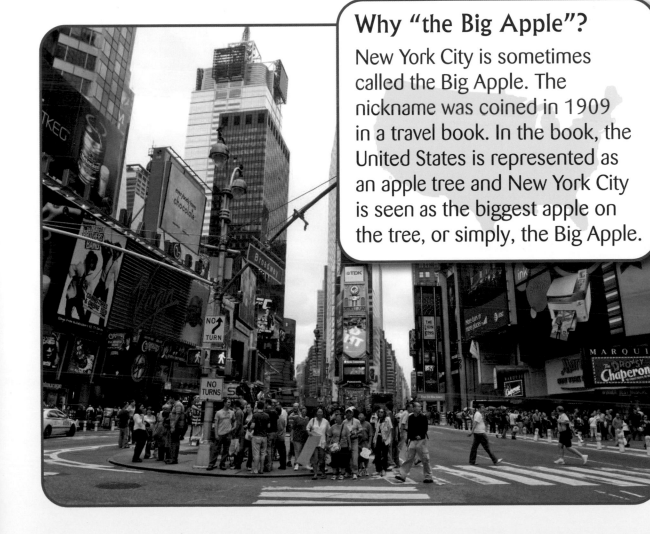

Why "the Big Apple"?

New York City is sometimes called the Big Apple. The nickname was coined in 1909 in a travel book. In the book, the United States is represented as an apple tree and New York City is seen as the biggest apple on the tree, or simply, the Big Apple.

Landforms

The Northeast region has a wide variety of landforms. Landforms are the natural surfaces that occur on Earth. The Northeast region is known for its wide variety of topography, or changes in elevation. It has many fresh lakes, rivers, mountains, **plateaus**, and coastal plains.

Ancient Appalachians

The Appalachians are an ancient mountain system that runs through parts of the Northeast region. They were formed over 470 million years ago and are the oldest mountains in North America. The Appalachian mountain **range** is called the Alleghenies in Pennsylvania and Maryland, the Catskills in New York, and the White Mountains in New Hampshire and Massachusetts.

Adirondack Mountains

The Adirondack mountain range runs through the state of New York. The Adirondacks are Dome Mountains. They were created by hot magma rising up from Earth's core and pushing or uplifting Earth's crust. Instead of erupting, as a volcano does, the magma cooled and became the inner core of the mountain.

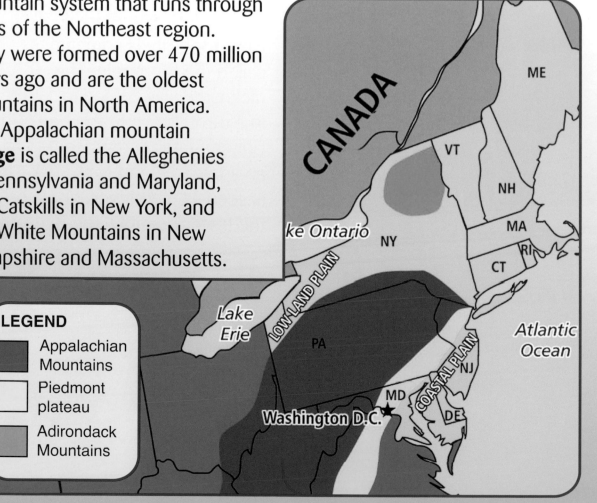

CANADA

ME

VT

NH

MA

RI

ke Ontario NY

CT

LOWLAND PLAIN

Lake Erie

PA

Atlantic Ocean

NJ

COASTAL PLAIN

MD

Washington D.C.

DE

LEGEND

Appalachian Mountains

Piedmont plateau

Adirondack Mountains

Plains

The Atlantic coastal plain lies east of the Appalachian mountain system. It is flat, level land that stretches from the mountains to the coast. The Lowland Plains are sometimes called the Central Plains. This landform lies west of the Appalachian Mountains. It is a flat area rich in soil and good for agriculture.

Uplands and Plateaus

The New England uplands are a landform of rolling hills, valleys, and mountains. It is located to the east of the Hudson River in the state of New York and continues through parts of Massachusetts, Connecticut, Maine, and Pennsylvania. A plateau is a raised area of flat land that is higher than one or more areas surrounding it. The Piedmont plateau is located east of the Appalachian mountain range, and west of the coastal plain. The Appalachian plateau is found west of the Appalachian mountain range.

Great Heights!

The tallest mountain peak in the Northeast region is Mount Washington in New Hampshire. It stands 6,288 feet (1,917 m) tall.

Mount Washington is the highest point in the Northeastern region.

It's a Waterful Region

The Northeastern states have great freshwater sources in its many lakes, streams, and rivers. These water sources provide natural transportation routes, **hydroelectric** power sources, and beautiful, scenic views for tourists. Most of the Northeastern states share a coastline on the Atlantic Ocean. Only two of the 11 Northeastern states, Vermont and Pennsylvania, are not on the coast of the Atlantic Ocean.

Niagara Falls attracts millions of tourists every year.

Niagara Falls

Niagara Falls are the two most powerful, natural waterfalls in North America. They are called the Horseshoe Falls and the American Falls. The Niagara River that feeds the falls is a natural, international border between New York State and Canada. The American Falls lie on the American side in the Northeastern state of New York. Niagara Falls was formed about 10,000 years ago by a massive glacier. It is the largest source of electricity for New York State.

Lakes

The Northeast region is home to many freshwater lakes. Two of the five Great Lakes, Lake Ontario and Lake Erie, border the Northeastern states of New York and Pennsylvania. Many smaller lakes, such as Mirror Lake, are found in the Northeastern states, too. Mirror Lake is the setting for the world famous village resort, Lake Placid, in New York State.

Rivers

Rivers begin on the top of a mountain. They are fed by fresh rainwater and melting snow. Rivers move fresh water toward larger bodies of water such as oceans. Major rivers in the Northeastern United States are the Hudson, Delaware, Connecticut, and Ohio.

Capes and Bays

A cape is a body of land that extends into a body of water. Cape Cod is a well known cape located in Massachusetts. Long Island is another cape on the Northeastern coast.

Estuaries

Chesapeake Bay is the largest estuary in the United States. An estuary is a coastal body of water that comes inland and is partially surrounded by land on both sides. It is connected to the ocean but is also fed by freshwater from rivers and streams.

River Apart

The St. Lawrence River is a natural border between part of the state of New York and Canada.

The Climate

People often choose to live in the Northeastern states because the climate fits their lifestyles. The northernmost parts of the region tend to have cool summers and mild winters. In the southernmost areas, they have warmer summers and colder winters.

Nor'easter

A Nor'easter is a storm that begins on the east coast of North America. It occurs when a cold air mass from the north clashes with a warm air mass from the southwest or over the Atlantic Ocean.

How Winds Affect Climate

Prevailing winds can cause changes to the Northeastern climate. Prevailing winds are global wind patterns that usually travel across an area. In the Northeastern region lies the boundary line for two wind patterns. The westerlies bring warm, humid air from the Gulf of Mexico and the polar easterlies bring cold, dry air from northern Canada. The weather can change quickly depending on which side of the boundary the area is on.

Nor'easters cause coastal flooding.

How Water Affects Climate

An area's closeness to a large body of water also affects the climate. Large bodies of water, such as the Atlantic Ocean or the Great Lakes, tend to absorb and store more heat energy than the air, which leaves the land around them cooler. When the temperatures become colder, the water releases its stored heat to nearby areas and makes the temperatures milder. The Great Lakes also cause the areas around them to get a lot of snow in winter. When cold winds from the north pass over the unfrozen Great Lakes, the winds are warmed by the lake's stored heat and pick up moisture. When the winds hit the colder land areas again they release their moisture in the form of snow.

Mountain Climate

A mountain's climate changes at different heights. Air cools as it rises and temperatures are colder at higher **altitudes**. Mountain areas also affect **precipitation**. Winds carry warm air masses up a mountain. Warm air holds moisture. As the warm air travels upward, the air cools and holds less precipitation. It then falls in the form of rain or snow.

Snow belt areas such as northern New York State get lake-effect snowfalls in the winter.

The First Peoples

The First Americans arrived around 30,000 years ago. Earth looked very different back then. Scientists believe these First Peoples traveled from Asia over a land bridge in present-day Alaska and moved into North America. Many of these First Peoples came to live in what is now the Northeast region of the United States. The two main Native American groups that lived in the Northeast spoke Algonquian or Iroquois. Different nations fell within one of these two groups.

Algonquian

Algonquian Native Americans speak Algonquian language. The name Algonquian means fishing with spears from canoes. The Algonquian people are part of the Abenaki, Penobscot, Wampanoag, and Delaware nations, and lived in the Northeast in the early 1600s. Algonquian Native Americans lived in dome-shaped wigwams. They lived in villages near the Great Lakes and in the Northeast's coastal areas.

(top) Northeastern Native Americans built birch-bark canoes for travel.

(left) Wigwams were one-family homes. They were built with young tree frames covered with bark or grasses.

Iroquois

Iroquois Native Americans speak Iroquois language. They belong to nations such as the Mohawk, Oneida, Onondaga, Cayuga, and Seneca. Iroquois means "people of the Longhouse." Iroquois families lived together in long, house-like structures in villages. Many Iroquois peoples lived in what are now the states of New York and Pennsylvania. Northeastern Native Americans farmed, fished, and hunted for their food. They used the Northeast's plentiful rivers, streams, and lakes as transportation routes.

European settlers

The arrival of European settlers changed the Native Americans' way of life. Many Native Americans died in battles with European settlers or from diseases the Europeans introduced to the area. In 1830, President Jackson introduced the Indian Removal Act which forced Native Americans to relocate further west so that European Americans could settle their land. The journey west was called the "Trail of Tears." Native Americans traveled hundreds of miles (km) with no shelter and very little food and water. Many caught diseases and died.

Many Iroquois families lived together in a longhouse.

Coming to America

European settlers from Great Britain landed on the Northeast coast in the early 1600s. They settled the first colony on the Northeast coast in Plymouth, Massachusetts. A colony is a group of people who have settled in a new area, but are still ruled by their homeland. The settlers called their new home New England, and the name is still used today.

The Original 13 Colonies

By the early 1700s, European **immigrants** had settled 13 colonies in America. Nine of these original colonies are found in the Northeast region. They are New Hampshire, Massachusetts, Rhode Island, Connecticut, New York, New Jersey, Pennsylvania, Delaware, and Maryland.

Ellis Island

Millions of immigrants came from Europe to America on ships. Most ships came to America through New York Harbor. In 1892, U.S. officials set up an immigration center at Ellis Island to control the health and number of immigrants entering the country. The immigrants had to pass a medical exam.

(bottom left) The Statue of Liberty has welcomed many new immigrants to Ellis Island in New York Harbor.

(bottom right) Today, many people visit the Ellis Island Immigration Museum to research their family's history.

African-Americans

The first African-Americans to arrive in America came against their will. In the mid-1600s, European slave traders brought African people to the British colonies in America and sold them into slavery. Slavery existed for hundreds of years in America. By the early 1800s, most Northeastern states no longer allowed slavery, but a number of Southeastern states still did. Some slaves ran away to the Northeastern states to live in freedom. Part of the reason that the United States fought the Civil War was over the issue of slavery. President Abraham Lincoln's Emancipation Proclamation promised freedom for all Americans from slavery. By January 1865, slavery was illegal in America.

(top) Slaves were forced to work long hours for no pay.

(bottom) The Emancipation Proclamation promised freedom from slavery.

First State to End Slavery

The first state to abolish slavery was the Northeastern state of Vermont in 1777.

Population Distribution

The geography of a region affects where people decide to live. Both Native Americans and early European settlers chose to live in the Northeastern region because of the land's geography. Hundreds of years later, it is still a highly populated area. Seventeen percent of the total U.S. population lives in the Northeastern states.

Location, Location, Location

The Northeast Atlantic Coast's naturally protected bays, harbors, and islands make it perfect for water transportation. Many large cities in the Northeast, such as New York, Boston, and Hartford were developed there for this reason. Inland from the coast, west of the coastal plain, the Piedmont fall line is formed of very old, hard rock. Where rivers flow over the fall line, falls and rapids are created which provided good sources of power for early industries. People were needed to operate the industries, so many moved to the area to find work.

Many large cities, such as New York City shown here, chose to build on large waterways for water transportation.

Largest cities

America's largest city in terms of population is New York City. Over eight million people live in the city and millions more live in the surrounding **suburbs**. Philadelphia is the fifth largest American city with almost two million people living there, and millions more in surrounding suburbs. Boston is the third-largest city in the Northeastern states with over 600,000 residents living there. What these three cities share in common is that they are all located on important waterways. New York City is surrounded by the Atlantic Ocean, New York Harbor, Hudson River, and the East River. Philadelphia is on the Delaware River, and Boston is on the Atlantic Coast.

Top Marks in Schools

The Northeastern region of the United States is home to the finest universities in America. The top four include Harvard University in Cambridge, Massachusetts, Princeton University in Princeton, New Jersey, Yale University in New Haven, Connecticut, and Columbia University in New York, New York. In fact, these universities are considered to be some of the finest in the world!

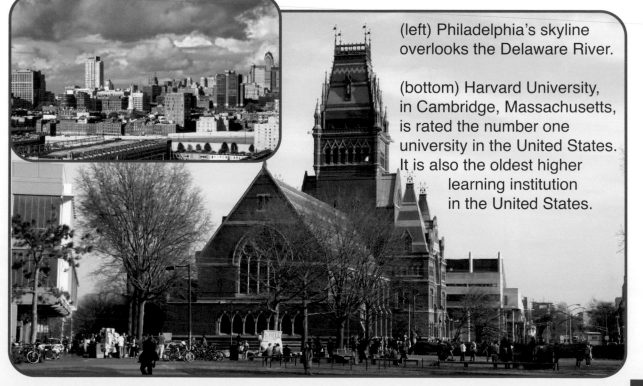

(left) Philadelphia's skyline overlooks the Delaware River.

(bottom) Harvard University, in Cambridge, Massachusetts, is rated the number one university in the United States. It is also the oldest higher learning institution in the United States.

Natural Resources

The Northeastern states are rich in natural resources. Natural resources are materials found in nature that can be made into products.

Sweet Vermont

The state of Vermont produces more maple syrup in the United States than any other state. Farmers tap into sugar maple trees in the springtime to collect the sap. The sugar maple tree is a state symbol of Vermont.

Something to "Wine" About

New York State is ranked third in wine production in the United States. Wine is made from grapes. Grapes are grown in areas near Lake Erie, the Finger Lakes, and Long Island.

Mining

Iron ore and coal were plentiful in Northeastern states such as Pennsylvania. During the 1800s, industries needed coal for energy to run machinery. Iron ore is needed to make steel. Pennsylvania was once the United States' leading producer of steel.

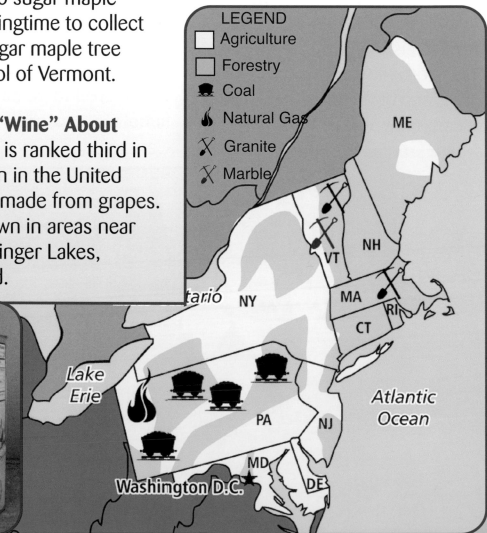

LEGEND
- ☐ Agriculture
- ☐ Forestry
- 🛒 Coal
- 🔥 Natural Gas
- ✗ Granite
- ✗ Marble

ME

NH

VT

MA

RI

CT

NY

Ontario

Lake Erie

PA

NJ

MD

DE

Washington D.C.

Atlantic Ocean

State of Vermont
PURE
MAPLE SYRUP

Dairy Belt

The Dairy Belt is located in the northernmost region of the United States that extends from the east coast to the west coast. Cows produce milk year-round in cooler climates. They are not suited for hot climates. The Northeastern states are part of the dairy belt because of the shorter growing season. The area has a cooler climate that is perfect for raising dairy cows and milk production.

Berry Good Region

The Northeastern state of Massachusetts is known for its cranberry crops. It is the second-largest cranberry producing state in the United States. Cranberries grow in marshes and bogs.

Marshes and bogs are soft, wet, spongy areas of land. Further north, states such as Maine are known for their blueberry production. Maine is the leading American state in wild blueberries. The crop brings in millions of dollars every year!

Seafood Industry

The Northeastern states, with its thousands of miles of seacoasts, are renowned for their seafood industry. Maryland's Chesapeake Bay supplies more crab than any other area in the United States. Maine and Massachusetts are famous for their lobster catches. Connecticut is known for its oyster industry.

(right) Many from Maine are employed in the seafood industry.
(below) Massachusetts is well known for its cranberry crops.

Economy and Industry

The industrial revolution began in the 1800s. It was a change in how products are manufactured, or made. Before the industrial revolution, products were made by hand or at home. The industrial revolution introduced machines to do work in factories that made products such as textiles and steel. Textiles are woven materials such as cloth. This meant many more products could be made in much less time. The Northeastern region of the United States was the perfect location for industries for many reasons. Industries needed fast-moving rivers and coal to power them. The rivers and waterways were also important to ship natural resources and products. Many skilled workers were needed to operate them. They needed natural resources to make products from, such as agriculture, lumber, and iron.

The Northeastern region met all the demands for these new industries. Today, industries in the Northeast produce electronics such as computers. They make products such as machinery, medicines, and processed foods.

(bottom) Slater Mill in Pawtucket, Rhode Island was built in 1793. It was the first water-powered, cotton spinning mill in North America.

Media Moguls

New York City is one of the world's most important media centers. Media are ways to communicate with everyone in the world, such as through books, records, newspapers, television, and movies. New York is home to the most important newspapers, and the biggest publishing and record companies in the world.

George Washington and Wall Street

George Washington took his oath of office at Federal Hall on Wall Street on April 30, 1789.

Wall Street

New York is also home to one of the world's most famous and largest **financial** centers called Wall Street. It is located in Lower Manhattan and is home to many financial businesses such as the New York Stock Exchange and the Federal Reserve Building. A stock exchange is a place where shares, or part ownership, in a company are bought and sold. Many banks and investment companies are also found on Wall Street.

Many tourists visit the historic New York Stock Exchange on Wall Street.

Tourism

The Northeast region's rich history attracts many visitors every year. The summer climate is more enjoyably cooler than the more southern states, and many vacation on the sunny, sandy beaches. In winter, the snowy mountains draw skiing and snowboarding enthusiasts. **Tourism** is one of the area's biggest industries. Tourism in New York City alone brought in billions of dollars in 2010!

New York, New York
Over 40 million people visit New York City every year. Times Square is one of the city's most popular tourist places. Colorful **billboards** light up the bustling street intersection in Manhattan. It is also the spot where millions watch the ball drop on New Year's Eve. The Statue of Liberty is a famous landmark in New York. It stands on Liberty Island in the New York Bay. Millions of tourists visit this symbol of American freedom. The Empire State Building is another tourist hotspot. In 2011, it was the tallest building in New

York City—but not for long. When the One World Trade Center—being built on the land that the World Trade Center once stood on—is completed it will be taller than the Empire State Building.

When the Empire State Building was built in1931 it was the world's tallest building.

Boston's Freedom Trail

Boston's Freedom Trail is a 2.5 mile red-brick walking trail. On this trail, tourists visit historical churches, houses, cemeteries, parks, and even a ship to learn about American history.

Philadelphia Freedom

Philadelphia, Pennsylvania, is one of the great historical cities of the United States. During the American Revolutionary War, Philadelphia was the capital of the newly formed United States of America. The Declaration of Independence was signed at Independence Hall in 1776. The United States Constitution was signed in the same hall in 1787.

America's Sailing Capital

Annapolis, Maryland, and Newport, Rhode Island, both claim to be the sailing capital of the United States. Annapolis, the capital city of Maryland, is located on Chesapeake Bay at the mouth of the Severn River. Newport is a city on Aquidneck Island in Narragansett Bay. Many tourists visit both historic seaports every year.

(top) This bustling Annapolis harbor sees thousands of sailing enthusiasts every summer.
(bottom) Tourists can visit Independence Hall (left) and other historical sites such as the Liberty Bell (right) at the 45-acre (18-hectare) Independence National Historical Park in Philadelphia.

The Northeastern Culture

Ethnic groups are people who have the same cultural **heritage**. They, or their relatives, came from the same country. Ethnic groups share things in common such as language, religion, and physical appearance. Americans proudly describe their country as a mosaic or salad bowl that has many different parts, or cultures. In the Northeastern region, people celebrate their culture and share their traditions with others at parades, food festivals, and music festivals that are held every year.

Carnival

Caribbean carnival parades are spectacular shows with bright, beautiful costumes worn by dancers in the parade. The Labor Day parade, also known as the West Indian Carnival, is always held on the first Monday in September in New York. The parade first began in Harlem in the 1920s, but has since moved to the Eastern Parkway in Brooklyn, New York.

The West Indian Carnival has been held annually in New York City for over 50 years.

26

National Cherry Blossom Festival

Washington, D.C. celebrates the National Cherry Blossom festival in the spring. The annual event began in the early 1900s when the Mayor of Tokyo, Japan gave the city of Washington, D.C. Japanese cherry trees to honor the friendship between the two countries. It is a two-week long festival that begins near the end of March and runs into April. It closes with a parade along Constitution Avenue in Washington, D.C. The Japanese community also holds the Sakura Matsuri Japanese Street Festival as part of this celebration.

Ethnic Communities

Many ethnic groups of immigrants that came to the United States choose to live together in communities. For this reason, neighborhoods with names such as Little Italy, Chinatown, and Barrios exist in large, Northeastern cities. These cultural neighborhoods have similar architectural styles, offer similar businesses, and specialize in restaurants that feature cultural foods. They are a little bit of the old country that these immigrants left behind when they moved to the United States. They also add different colors and flavors to the American mosaic.

(left) Many large cities, such as New York pictured here, have Chinatowns and other cultural neighborhoods.
(below) The queens of the National Cherry Blossom Festival ride on a float in the annual parade held in Washington, D.C.

Art, Architecture, and Famous People

The Northeast region is proud of their rich, cultural heritage. People from the Northeast have been influenced by their homeland. And, in turn, they have influenced America and the world in the arts, architecture, and literature.

Modern Art

The 1913 Armory Show in New York City changed the way Americans thought about art. The international art exhibit brought modern works of art from European artists to the United States for the first time. Many people were shocked by the art forms such as cubism. The show influenced American artists to create their own modern works of art.

Architecture

Architecture is the design style of buildings. Many early homes and churches in the Northeastern states were influenced by architectural styles from Great Britain. One of these styles known as the Georgian style, was named after King George who had ruled England. Georgian style churches have tall, cone-shaped steeples and tall windows. A Georgian style home had a door in the center with a triangular crown overtop. Multi-pane windows were symmetrical.

The White House, home of the American president, is an example of a Georgian style home.

Benjamin Franklin

Benjamin Franklin was a famous Northeastern American who was one of the founding fathers of America. He was also a printer, writer, librarian, inventor, and politician. He was born in Boston, Massachusetts, and lived in Philadelphia, Pennsylvania. Benjamin opened the first public library in the United States. He invented bifocal glasses that let people see both near and far, and invented the first odometer that measured distances.

Born in the U.S.A.

Singer/songwriter Bruce Springsteen, or the "Boss" as he is often called, was born in the Northeastern state of New Jersey. Springsteen's album, called "Born in the U.S.A.," sold 15 million copies in the United States and was one of the best-selling albums of all time. He has won 20 Grammy Awards and was inducted into the Rock and Roll Hall of Fame in 1999.

(top) Benjamin Franklin (left) signed the Declaration of Independence, written in 1776.

(bottom) People around the world listen to Bruce Springsteen's music.

Harriet Beecher Stowe

A Connecticut woman named Harriet Beecher Stowe, wrote the famous novel *Uncle Tom's Cabin* in 1852. Her novel, written about the injustice of slavery, sold over 300,000 copies in its first year of print.

Timeline

35,000,000 B.C. – A giant meteorite falls from the sky and creates Chesapeake Bay.

28,000 B.C. – First Peoples arrive in North America. Scientists believe they walked across a land bridge that once existed between Asia and North America.

21,000 B.C. – Laurentian glacier deposits rocks and earth to create Cape Cod and other moraines in the Northeastern region.

8000 B.C. – Movements of large glaciers carve out Niagara Falls, Great Lakes, and smaller lakes in the Northeastern region.

1620 – European colonists arrive from Great Britain to settle the first colony in Plymouth, Massachusetts.

1625 – Dutch settlers come to settle New Netherland, which is New York City today.

1776 – The Declaration of Independence is signed in Philadelphia, Pennsylvania.

1777 – The state of Vermont becomes the first state to abolish slavery.

1787 – The United States Constitution is signed in Philadelphia, Pennsylvania.

1793 – Massachusetts inventor, Eli Whitney, invents the cotton gin.

1830 – The American government passes the Indian Removal Act of 1830, pushing Native Americans from their land to the West.

1852 – Harriet Beecher Stowe publishes her novel, *Uncle Tom's Cabin*, in the United States. It becomes the second best-selling book (following the Bible) in America in the 1800s.

1865 – Abraham Lincoln's Emancipation Proclamation promises all Americans freedom from slavery.

1886 – The Statue of Liberty is given to the United States from France.

1892 – U.S. officials open up an immigration center on Ellis Island in New York Harbor.

1913 – American artists welcome the International Art Exhibit called the 1913 Armory Show in New York City. This show begins the modern art movement for American artists in the United States.

1955 – New York City native, Jonas Salk, develops the polio vaccine.

1939 – Fallingwater, a house designed by Frank Lloyd Wright, is built in Pennsylvania. It later becomes a museum.

1965 – Immigration and Nationality Act allows more immigrants of all different nationalities to move to America.

1999 – New Jersey native, Bruce Springsteen, is inducted into the Rock and Roll Hall of Fame.

2011 – The Empire State Building is still the tallest building in New York City. It will be bumped from this spot when the One World Trade Center is completed in New York City.

Find Out More

BOOKS

Ethnic America: The Northeastern States by D. J. Herda, Millbrook Press, 1991.

The United States Region by Region by Patricia Kummer, Steck-Vaughn, 2002.

The Very First Americans by Cara Ashrose, Grosset & Dunlap, 1993.

WEBSITES

Find out more about the northeast region and America's other regions at:
www.eduplace.com/ss/socsci/tx/books/bkd/ilessons/

Discover everything you need to know about America's 50 states at:
www.factmonster.com/states.html

Learn about individual state flowers, flags, famous people, and more at this interesting site:
http://www.50states.com/

Glossary

altitude A measurement of height above sea level

billboard A large panel or screen used to advertise a product

border The outer edge, or outer limit, of an area

climate The average weather conditions of an area

colonize To form a colony, or settlement

financial Related to the management of money or other valuables

heritage Traditions that are passed on from generation to generation

hydroelectric To produce electricity from gathering the energy from moving water

immigrant A person who leaves one country to live in another country

plateau A flat, raised area of land

precipitation Water that falls to Earth's surface, such as rain or snow

range A group of mountains that were made at the same time by the same process

seaport A harbor that allows sea-going ships to come and go

subregions The subdivision, or smaller part, of a region

suburb A residential area or community that lies outside of a large city

tourism Traveling for pleasure

Index

Adirondack mountains 8

agriculture 9, 15, 20, 22

Appalachian mountains 8, 9

Atlantic Ocean 4, 6, 10, 12, 13, 18, 19

cities 6, 7, 18, 19, 23, 24, 25, 26, 27, 28

climate 4, 5, 12–13, 21, 24

culture 5, 26, 27, 28–29

European settlers 7, 15, 16, 18

food 15, 21, 22, 26, 27

immigrants 16–17, 27

industries 18, 20, 21, 22, 24

lakes 8, 10–11, 13, 14, 15, 20

Mid-Atlantic states 6

mountains 8, 9, 11, 13, 24

Native Americans 14, 15, 18

natural resources 5, 20–21, 22

New England 6, 9, 16

New York City 7, 18, 19, 23, 24, 26, 27, 28

rivers 8, 9, 10–11, 15, 18, 19, 22, 25

tourism 24–25